The Race Is On

The Race Is On

Kiptoo Kibet

EXCELLER BOOKS™
A GLOBAL PRESS

The Race Is On

Cover design by Exceller Books using resources from Pixabay.com

ISBN: 978-81-19524-75-4

First published in India in 2024 by Exceller Books

Address: G1, Dream Apartment, Degree College Road, Belgharia, Kolkata, 700056, India

EXCELLER BOOKS™
A GLOBAL PRESS

www.excellerbooks.com

Dedication

It is my great pleasure to dedicate this book to my family, especially my beloved wife, Gladys Kiprotich, who has always remained supportive towards my dream.

Acknowledgement

I wish to acknowledge the almighty God for enabling me to write this book. I also acknowledge my close friends and relatives for their endless moral support throughout the process.

Special thanks go to the following:

Mr. John Morrow-Smart bloger.com
Mr. Jonah kiprotich Tomno
Mr. Jonathan Kiprop

Table of Contents

The Race

Running in the race is for all but one win
All gather in a race with the passion to win
At the start of a race, all are winners
At the end of a race, one is the winner
At the end of a race, one goes away with gold
At the end of a race, one will be celebrated by many

At the beginning of the race, thousands stand as winners
No one registers in a race to lose
You enrol to win; you run to win
None can declare a winner in a race
Only God knows who will win the race
Even the very weak ones register to win

Are you planning for a race? Are you in a race?
Go ahead; maintain your thoughts, passion, and effort.
The race is neither for the swift nor strong nor wealthy
Time and chance come to them all.
Amidst thousands, you are one of the winners
Today you are last, tomorrow at bronze, next silver, then gold
You lose hope; you lose all in life
You lose all; you lose a life—
Run to finish the race and win tomorrow, if not today.

Purpose of Life

Greatest strategy is not dead in life but life without purpose
Life without purpose no difference, life without difference no hope
Life without hope is meaningless Meaningless life no difference
In God, a yearning life for difference
Difference difference, heave a sigh

Acknowledge God
Without God no purpose
Without purpose a meaningless life, Meaningless life stagnated man
Stagnated man despair awaits old age; all ends up in unproductive life
Trust God for wisdom and understanding
Difference difference heave, a sigh.

But what is life?
I define life as a marathon; I delay others to go
I define as a puzzle, I bow head like praying mantis all-day
I define life as a race; I overspeed and fall off track
I define it as just party I malinger and wander with bad companies.
Life is a test, and trust in God, With God all in all a yearning heart for difference.
Difference difference, heave a sigh.

Decision making
Making a difference begins with you

Be who you are, not who others are. Man's anguish is himself.
Man's toil is man's anguish; Man's toil is man's niche.
Man's niche is man's joy.
Self-esteem and actualization all equate to personality, and I deal
Difference difference, heave a sigh.

The Human Powerhouse

Like a strong pillar in a house
Who can do without me?
A weak pillar a week house
A pillar doesn't just count, but its content
The content determines the strength
Any hardwood is really hard and strong
Softwood is soft and weak

Talk of the human brain
The nervous system connectivity
The stronger and healthier the neurons are
The sharper the human brain
Reason out its shape and content
For all bodily functions, it takes the brain
For good survival, it takes the brain
For quick resolution, it takes the brain

Uniqueness of Man

Is man a unique organism?
Is man a creature?
Is the man superior?
Is man an animal?
Why a creature
Why a superior creature
As a potter of clay

The reason for man and other creatures
Why don't animals equate man in the brain?
What would the world be without man?
Without a creator, creatures won't exist.
Without a creator, man wouldn't exist.
The co-creator is man.
The holy ordained is man.
The worshiper is man
Creature dominions are man
Creature destruction is man

Individual Differences

I trust who I am before all
My talent is my inner resource
My character is my being
My interest is my trait; my trait is my aptitude
My aptitude, my enthusiasm, my daily gear
My character is my thoughts, my thoughts my speeches
Am I who the creator made?

You are tall and short; you are...I am...
You are brown, I am black, you are...I am...
You are genius I am average, you are eloquent I am disgusting
A social you antisocial me, A cheerful you autistic me
Patient you, I impatient. I am faster; you are slower; I am
Caution: you are careless. I am
Are we who God made?

Why are humans different?
All the creator's images but different personalities
You de-individuate you are guilt
You impersonate you are judged
Personal dejection no self-esteem
No self-esteem no confidence
No confidence personal condemnation
Personal condemnation image withdrawal
You are who you are and will be
Are you who God Made?

Sanguine

Sanguine sanguine
I am a sanguine
I am fearfully and wonderfully made
I am outgoing, a steady trait
A critical, calm thinker
Armchair psychologist
Contended and subject to stoic factor
I am extroverted, changeable
I am normal none, neurotic
My stature my instinct
Happy heart happy smile
Happy smile happy people
Happy people my applause
My congruence my delight
My beauty my happiness
My achievement my happiness
I resemble God my creator
I am who I am and should be

Melancholic

I am semi-melancholic choleric
Melancholic choleric psyche
I am fearfully and wonderfully made
General intelligence entails my instinct
Who can check my side?
I am unshakeable by the creature but the creator
My hardiness my personality
Histrionic, pessimistic to obscured scenes
I am passionate and anxious for an immediate niche
A quick resolute thinker
Always a friend in good
Disquieted in humiliation
I party with congruent and egocentric
A stiff-necked in a, fixed mind
My nature my personality
My personality my stature
My stature my beauty
My beauty my treasure
I resemble God my creator
I am who I should be!

Growth Mindset

I am the I before the us
We follow what I say
We feel what I feel
Who are we?
Who am I?
As a human, a simple computer
I am the central processing unit
Body parts like hands, stomach, and legs are the ones we
When I am on I am cautious
When I am in growth I am open to experience
When I am in growth I am creative
When I am in growth I am conscientious
When I am in growth I am agreeable
When I am in growth I am intelligent
When I am in growth I am realistic
When I am in growth I am an adventurer
When I am in growth I am productive
When I am in growth I am hardworking
When I am in growth I am decisive
I say I am okay, and they say we are okay

The Fixed Mindset

I am a well-set human, a simple computer
I depend on commands
I am always set to go
I always wait for the clapper
Who am I?
Fixed mind fixed mind, worst of a man
When I am fixed I am reserved
When I am fixed I am dopey
When I am fixed I am disorganized
When I am fixed I am dormant
When I am fixed I am unruly
When I am fixed I am unrealistic
When I am fixed I am lazy
When I am fixed I undeceive
When I am fixed I am rigid
When I am fixed I am prone to stagnation
When I am fixed I am abhorrent to the we
When I am fixed I am dependent
I say I am not okay; they are not okay

Perception

A twinkle of an eye
A chance to think out,
A chance to think
A chance to see
A chance to see
A chance to reveal
A chance to reveal
A chance to understand

What do you see? What do you hear?
What do you think? What do you know?
What do you understand? What do you feel?
Are your thoughts true?
I see negatively; you see positively
I see negatively, I see negatively
I fail to plan for it,
I fail to plan for success; I plan to fail myself,
What you think, you see, what you see, you hear
What you see, hear, will believe
What you believe you do, what you do, you are.

Do you see fortunes or misfortunes?
Do you see success or failures?
Do you see it tomorrow or today?
Be like a giraffe; get fresh and clean bread!

They Were

You see them they are new
You hear them; they are new
You do them; they are new
You do them; they are new
They happen to you; they are new
But they were there before you
They are strange, they are unbelievable
They are unbelievable they are unbearable
They are unbearable they are impossible
You renovate and rename them
They become new to you and others
But they were there before you.

Strange happens to occur, and history begins
You had never seen; they have seen
You have heard they had never heard
You ask why it happens and how,
You see bad things you curse; they see and welcome
They exist; they existed before you
Under the sun nothing is new
Man becomes new to events, situations, and circumstances
They were there before you were born and will be
Generation by generation, history repeats itself
A man stumbles on strange happenings
But they were there before him.

Thinking

Think big things to be big
Do you think you think?
Do you think of things you think of?
Do you think to think?
Beginning to think is thinking.
Thinking of something is the genesis.
Thinking is hard thinking is good.
The value of thinking is in your actions
Do you think you can stop thinking?
As you think to stop thinking you are thinking
What do you think of, gold or silver?
Why do you think of that thing?
Thinking, thinking is a response to your soul
The inner man speaks, desires and responds
You see to think, you hear to think
You think to learn you learn to know
You know to understand
You understand to act to be wise.

Wisdom

Be with a wise man; test him
Come close to a wise man
Relate with a wise man
Listen to a wise man; become wise
Become wise and have an understanding
Wisdom and understanding are gold
Wisdom and understanding make a good name
A good name is better than wealth
It brings good relations with others
Like a gentle answer from a wise man
Wisdom and understanding bring wealth.

Listen to a fool, follow him
Folly is the order of the day
A foolish man not only troubles himself
Havoc storms whole community
Be with a fool; get bonded like a tick on a cow
Laziness entails your actions
Follow a fool choose foolishness
Choose foolishness to become a deject to wise ones
Become a deject become hopeless
Become hopeless become manic
Become manic and lose dignity
Lose dignity a mockery to God

Man As a Moral Agent

Why, man, why a moral agent is?
Being human does not need to be an animal
Being an animal does not need to be human
Instinctive brain and stature correlate with humans and animals
Humans and animals possess consciousness
Possess thinking but degree matters
Humans are so dominant in brain content
Brain functioning is superior
The man knows right and wrong; He differentiates good and bad
Man is superior in thinking; Man acts as a source of evil
Man is God's co-creator

The nature of personality makes us incongruent
Cultural diversions dictate our morality
The normal, normal abnormal and abnormal normal
All as the setting of culture and personality
Morality and immorality are always incoherent
Morality and immorality are only to be or not to
In concurrent or in concurrent with culture and personality,
Man is a well-destined creature
Created and meant to act like God
Meant to be subject to God, Meant to be wise, and think clearly
Meant to implement God's commands
Meant to be superior on land
Meant to choose between right and wrong
Meant to be punished for wrong and rewarded in good

Men before God

I am a human you are a human, you are human they are human
They are human we are human, we are human we are creatures
We are creatures; we belong to the Creator,
We belong to the Creator; we are like the Creator
We are like creators, we are special, we are special, we are responsible
We are meant to obey, worship, and procreate
Being like God means holiness; we are meant to love each other

A human is a human, God remains God
God's creature remains his
I am beautiful; you are beautiful
He is handsome; you are handsome
We are like God
I am ugly; you are ugly
God remains God
In his likeness he made us; we are like God; we are like God
I call you ugly I mock God; you call me ugly you mock God
We mock God. We are silly; who is ugly, and who is beautiful?
Is God's image not one? What a puzzle; are we one?
Who is smart enough to judge God's creation? What are we proud of?
Be proud and boast of God than yourself
Whoever hates man hates God; whoever hates God is not wise
Whoever mistreats man reckons with God
Whoever reckons with God deserves punishment

Any evil act towards man is a war against God
No war against God will succeed.

Life As a Wheel

A wheel a stationed machine
A wheel a flexible machine
A step by step a spindle wheel
A spindle wheel is a progress
A clockwise anticlockwise
A clockwise way forward
Anticlockwise, a way backward
Life as a wheel a rider needed
A rider for your own?
A good rider, are you?
Your life is your wheel.
Your wheel your choice
A good wheel enjoyable riding
A good wheel is costly to get
Psychologically, physically and emotionally
You think you feel you hear
A good wheel that is easier to use but hard to make
A journey to the peak
A wheel to push
A wheel to push a need to make
A need to make a strategy needed

The Need Hierarchy

A need is a need
A want is a want
Luxury is a luxury
You have a need
He has a want
You have needs and wants, and they have the luxury
Food and a car are basic
Love and shelter one is a physical need
The urgency we need the hierarchy
The hierarchy is the order of desires
A luxurious car without food is folly
A lavish lifestyle without basics is madness
A need is a need a want is a want

Infinity of Needs

Talk of satisfaction and begin thinking
Are human needs fully meet once?
Yes, now I am not hungry tomorrow, I am
I get food, I think of clothing
I get plenty of food. I think of high-class eats
I get the gentle dress. I think of a more eloquent one
Food comes shelter comes, clothing comes
I say I am not hungry; I am clothed, sheltered
Next, am I safe? Another is that I am beautiful.
Am I handsome and a full man?

Infinity infinity infinity
Tell me how to fully satisfy your needs, or I will tell you why you cannot do it.
Human-like any other living organism, a need to survive a need to grow
A couple of needs are always infinite; a need is a constant variable
A constant variable flexible means to meet
You have it today to fullest tomorrow you need
You earn more money to make you need more
You need more money to make you work harder
You get basic needs; you need more complex
You need more complex all at infinite
You get basics; you need safety; you get basics; you need love
You get the love you need, self-esteem
You get self-esteem, but you need actualization
Infinity infinity of human needs
Who and how can it be fully met once?

Desires Are Man's Dilemmas

Man's desires are incoherent
He desires to be happy you desire to be rich
They desire to be united; you desire to separate
He desires to prosper all you desire to prosper alone
Men are inherent in thoughts
Personality equates desires
You are egocentric; you are alone
They desire holistically they are together
Desires are endless and changeable
You desire this today that tomorrow
They desire that today the other tomorrow
Desires unfixed in nature
Desires a critique to satisfy
Desires in consciousness
Desires in unconsciousness
Man desires before demanding
Man demands after knowing and seeing
Man toils towards his desires

The Deadline

Deadline for all ends for all
The end of all beginning for all
The deadline for anxiety
The anxiety the rush
The rush the crush
The crush the dislocation
Deadline for all ends for all
I infer I concur with it all
The deadline for the affixed
The affixed consistency
The consistency and coherence
Deadline for all ends for all

The deadline for all ends for all
Always tuned to accomplishment
Tuned to the accomplishment of punctuality
Punctuality entails efficiency
As efficient you are accurate you are
Always on deadline always awake
Always awake, always active
Without accurate deadline no order
No order greater confusion
Great confusion great errors
Deadline for all ends for all.

A Morsel or Full Bread?

Little by little fills a tin
Morse…morsels make full bread
You want it full and reject even a better morsel
Ambitious but pessimistic and selective
The other one picks whatever comes
Gathers quick goodies quickly and quietly
Waiting while wasting willingly will you
His basket is full of bread morsels, and yours is empty
Who is shrewd, a morsel or a full bread?

Your Good Day My Bad Day

Good day bad day
All days are the same; what a day entails varies
Your thrill, your good day
My disgust my bad day
What makes Monday bad, and what makes Thursday bad?
What makes Friday good?
Our disillusioned, clouded minds, our confused, confusion
The confusion confuses the fixed mind and the growth mind
Routine routine, a boredom workplace
Boredom workplace bad times count
Bad time counts, bad day's counts
Intrinsic motivation dictates a tuned mind
A tuned mind and a growth mindset
A growth mindset a passion for diligent work
Passion for work is love for all days

Am I bewitched?
As Monday approaches, the scratch of butterflies in my stomach
Bondage to situations, Phobic to daily routine
Another hell of day's unexpected situations
You are partying I am mourning
You live to it I live to lament, you are lavishing I am pegging
You live I live, you are excellent I am poor
You live, I live; you are healthy I in intensive care
Life remains in all situations; what matters is how it takes us.

Regrets

Regret and remain humiliated
Remain humiliated and demotivated
Remain demotivated and become your own obstacle
Own obstacle own destructor
You regret you criticize
You criticize; you are suspicious
Be suspicious lose friends
Lose friends nagging begins
Regrets regrets, what cause?

For what reason do regrets exist?
A desire comes, and action is taken.
Action taken causes regrets.
A change of desire a change of mind
Even in allegations regrets exist
A wish comes after an event
Under the sun unfairness exist
As others regret others rejoice
As others are troubled others celebrate.

Regret regrets an endless blink
Endless struggle futile desire
You ask why you
You ask how you
They have done to you
It has happened to you

The Suffering Soul

Suffering suffering, my soul cry
I am blocked and deterred by sickness, by misfortune
The world around becomes a wild beast
Gnashing teeth and salivating for me
First, though I was born with six fingers
Born with six fingers but now siege
Context of suffering amidst hungry vultures
Short vulnerability a flash of obsolescence, a flash of obsolescence, a flash of stagnation
A flash of stagnation a flash of despair

Humanity's hindsight reveals a progress
That vitality is sign generativist, and generativist ensure integrity
Suffering suffering, I am weary enough
Who can see and answer my tears?
Keep heart, darling, a better living dog than a dead lion
A good future awaits you despite bad nick
Try hope and optimism for rejuvenation,
Every being has a hay day and a put-down

Your hardiness, your defence
Your confession your power of decision, Power of decision dictates life
You confess the life you choose to live; you confess death you decide to die
You decide to die you surrender, you surrender you are overwhelmed

You are overwhelmed you wait to die; you die Satan gains you lose
You confess life; you resist death; you resist deadly; you accept to live
You accept to live, you believe to live, you live, Satan loses, you gain
You are on a journey of several jungles; you journeyman change direction, not destiny!
They say that but who can withstand
Suffering, suffering, I am weary enough
Who can see my tears and hear my cry?

Happiness

Happiness happiness, where is it?
You say a happy man is a wealthy man, but do riches make a man happy?
Be authentic and speak logic; how many affluent men are in anguish?
Full of stress depression, anxiety, toiling
The more I have the more I desire for many, the more the desires the more the stress
The little I have the more I worry for tomorrow's bread
Under the sun is trouble with confused creatures.
Man, man, the likeness of God
Why defy God's counsel? I ask myself
I am egocentric and thinking of being independent
My happiness is accomplishing my desires
Rich ones get to their luxuries but strangers take away
Poor ones work under pressure all day but are paid little or not
These things are senseless under the sun
What can make man happy?
When and how can a man make himself happy?
Were we made as subjects of torment?
Happiness happiness, where is it?

The young say happy are the old who have eaten much salt
That they have tasted and enjoyed the world
They wish to live and grow old like them, yet regret of old age is felt
They think they have no stress but are stressed about dying and leaving wealth

The stress of unaccomplished visions in life, the stress of life after death

A wise man listens to God, who gives happiness
He gets contended with possession
Toils for daily bread not anxiety for riches
Better to die at birth than a man who sees the world but does not enjoy
For when he dies, no one remembers; his riches vanish.
Happiness happiness, where is it?

Social Interaction

From one place to another, you find
From one group to another you form
From one status to the other, you achieve
From one age to the other, you clock
In every stage, you enjoy groups of interaction
Socialists say we meet and share
Functionalists say we meet and compete
We meet for events to interact
People Move Mountains do not
You are new to me; I am new to you
A nice smile opens the heart
A soft tongue attracts the heart
New interaction, the social network begins
We become friends; we share ideas
We share ideas, we share efforts
We share the efforts we develop

Family, the grass root of social interaction
Institution the primary agent of interaction
Sports the secondary agent
Communities form societies
Societies form states
Sates form continents
Continents combine the world

Your Meat Is Someone's Poison

Your friend can be my enemy
My enemy can be your friend
Your enemy can be my enemy
Your friend can be my friend
Who are you am I to you?

I love you to love me
They hate you hate me
Revenge to you, revenge to me
Your happiness my happiness
Your misfortune my misfortune
Your people my people
Your company my company
Who are you am I to you?

Man and Woman

A man is a man
A woman is a woman
Man and woman all human
Human is human
Man the family head
Woman home builder
Man the community head
Women are the men's backup

Women the builders
Men the forerunners
Who is the best who is special?
Concrete and cement mix to make a block
As man and woman's effort for a strong pillar
Is cement and concrete the same?
You say no, and I say yes
What domain product is it from cement and concrete?

Maize is maize, but different end products
Corn oil is a different thing; Maize flour is a different thing
Corn oil, maize flour all maize product
A woman from man's rib, A woman is man's flesh
Then what a man, woman, a real man by dignity
Is not a woman part of man, man, and woman one image
One image one pillar, Building a home building a community
Building a community building a nation,
Building a nation-building the world
Are you a man or a woman? Then be!

Morality

Assertion assertion assertion man to live
Be different, be different be different; you live
Come, come we talk come we speak sense
Where does sexual immorality come from?
Where does adultery come from?
Where does divorce come from?
Where does domestic violence come from?
Unfaithfulness unfaithfulness to God
Disobedience to God, God says one man one woman
Abstinence before marriage, faithfulness in marriage
Fornication, fornication, body lust, body lust.
Without God's revival immorality and death on the rise
Without God, life sways like a flag.

Back I up us make the difference
For your future and generation to come
Self-control from God by the Holy Spirit
Never struggle, but trust God
One song, one song for difference
If married, sing with me the initial B
Be faithful, be faithful, be faithful you to live.
If not married, sign initial A,
Abstinence abstinence abstinence you to live
Be different be different be different you to live
In Jesus in Jesus in Jesus you to live.

Man Is People

I was at vantage and saw them down; I was at vantage and saw me high
Saw me high praised me, Praised me I boasted
I boasted, became stupid and Became stupid, and defied correction
Defied correction, became blind insight
Became blind and dug my own grave daily
Became lavish; I was lavished
I thought I was unshakeable mountain
The world looked small; I was a king
I saw the poor I saw their fault, I saw the sick saw their making
I saw their challenges I saw their failures
I thought I was unshakeable mountain.

Common sense uncommon to me
I dug and delved into my own grave; I mocked the destitute
I ignored orphans and disabled
I thought life was immortal thought wealth was everlasting
I thought I was unshakeable mountain.

But gosh! Man is people; I am fading!
I look for a shilling like a donkey's horn
I dig hard rock to get a single meal
A selfish hay day a selfish incident, I am hopeless like destitute
From early morning to late evening, I sit outdoors from sunrise and onset
Like a praying mantis, I lament insight

I am crushing like a foolish man's house in a swamp
I cry for help, but no one listens
I thought I was unshakeable mountain.

Vengeance

Vengeance vengeance was mindless; they are
I am deserted like an old beehive
I was famous for suits cars but Now in racks and walking sticks
I thought I was and could be at vantage forever
I became rich, ignored others
Even the very empowerment I could not do
I loved seeing others pegging
I loved seeing other desperate
I loved the rich and ignored the poor.
Friends, friends, hear this;
Be rich make others rich,
Man is people; Man is society; Man is people; people are man!
My grave is maturing and will enter poor
Thought I had enough but where are they
Thought I was a king, but now a cowboy
I exploited many without mercy; now they do to me
I had no mercy for the destitute; now none has mercy for me
Who can tell me why rich and poor should be a compliment?
I thought I was the overall king, but now I am a cowboy.

The Tongue

Small but drives a man to hell
Small but control life
A good tongue a good speech
A tongue tastes a tongue utters
A tongue curses a tongue blesses
Whoever controls his tongue controls his life
Like a flame in dry grass
A bad tongue stirs up anger
A good tongue sweeps away anger
A wise man speaks wise words
A folly man speaks out of foolishness
The tongue reveals the inner man
Without the tongue, there would be no gossip
No gossip means good relations
Good relations mean peace and harmony

The tongue, a small organ but poisonous
Poisonous if no control, healer in good control
Well-spoken words bring applauds to the human heart
The tongue a good communicator, Bad or good it does all
It protects the human soul if it is good and destroys the human soul if it is bad
The goodness of man the heart, the test the tongue
Words spoken never return or cease
One word made many by many
I say this: you report that he reports the other

Another Man

Another man another man
Another man is rich, another man is poor
Another man is weak; another man is strong
Another man is a king; another man is a servant
When rich man spit he spit wealth when poor man spit he spit poverty
A rich man speaks nonsense and is heard when a poor man speaks sense nobody hears
Nobody listens to the poor wise man; nobody honours the poor man
A rich, foolish king speaks to the whole society and echoes
A wise poor man speaks to the rich and shut them down

Another man another man
Another man is wise; another man is dull
Do riches make us wise or does wisdom make us rich?
Do riches equate to respect?
The poor man is subject to respect; the rich man is to give order
The poor man is a servant to the rich,
The poor man is to be submissive
The poor and rich men are dependent

Another man another man
He is suppressed but has no voice; He is mistreated but really destitute
The hardest working under the sun,
He is directed to dig his grave, He is ordered to burry himself
Poor man's hay day is pleasing his boss
Another man is wise another man is dull
Another man is rich another man is poor
Who are you under the sun?

The End of a Matter

Another one begins well and ends well
Another one begins well and ends in pain
Another one begins bad and ends well
Another one begins bad and ends badly
Everything with a start has its end
To start is easy but to end is hard
The end of a matter is better than its beginning

An idea yields a vision; a vision is a dream.
A dream yields an urge; an urge yields a plan
A plan yields actions that yield activities
Amidst obstacles the end of a matter is paramount
Every action has its end no matter the beginning
To start is easy but to end is hard
The end of a matter is better than its beginning

www.ingramcontent.com/pod-product-compliance
Lightning Source LLC
Chambersburg PA
CBHW050026170726
48282CB00025B/567
* 9 7 8 8 1 1 9 5 2 4 7 5 4 *